Love's Crocheted Dress

Written by: Michelle Lynae

ISBN: 9798597522128
Copyright © 2021 Michelle L. Clark
All Rights Reserved

Written by Michelle L. Clark   Illustrations by Kerrie Hubbard   Edited by Nina Marie Thomas

This rhyme is dedicated to my mother,
and her love for us
woven through a little crocheted dress.

Also, to my sisters
who complete
our three-stranded cord.

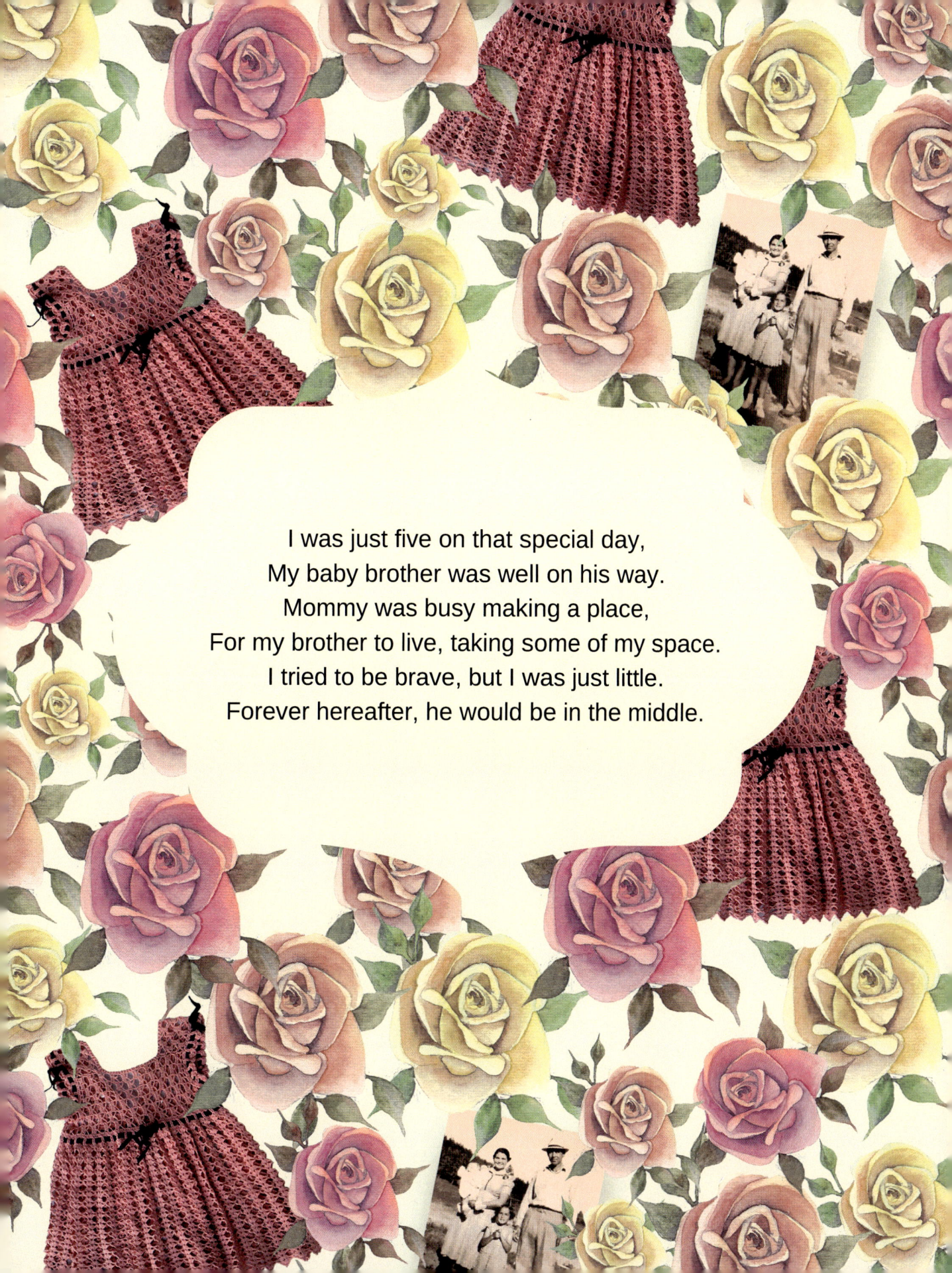

I was just five on that special day,
My baby brother was well on his way.
Mommy was busy making a place,
For my brother to live, taking some of my space.
I tried to be brave, but I was just little.
Forever hereafter, he would be in the middle.

I knew how to share, but would learn even more...
When a gentle knock came, and we opened the door.
I was not forgotten, left out, and not hidden.
It was composed of slipped stitches, loops and black ribbon.
She thought of me, with this gift in her hand,
The sweetest crocheted dress in all the land!

Mommy loved the dress too, keeping it safe as can be,
But I wanted to share the special love shown to me.
So, friends and cousins, felt that love oh so strong.
Years later she told me, "Oh cousin, you're wrong!"
That beautiful dress was not for just you,
That dress was not coral, that dress was pale blue!

My neighbor next door was like another grandmother.
Her daughter was grown, so her love spilled out to others.
She spent many months crocheting the dress,
In the softest of coral, every stitch was her best.
Black velveteen ribbon, when in the mirror I'd pose,
Softly ran through my fingers, like petals of a rose.

We each felt so special, beautiful, and bright.
Like a fair maiden or princess, forever just right.
Faces lit up while dancing a twirl,
This dress touched the heart of each little girl.
Whenever I donned her, I felt like a queen.
Little did I know what this would all grow up to mean...

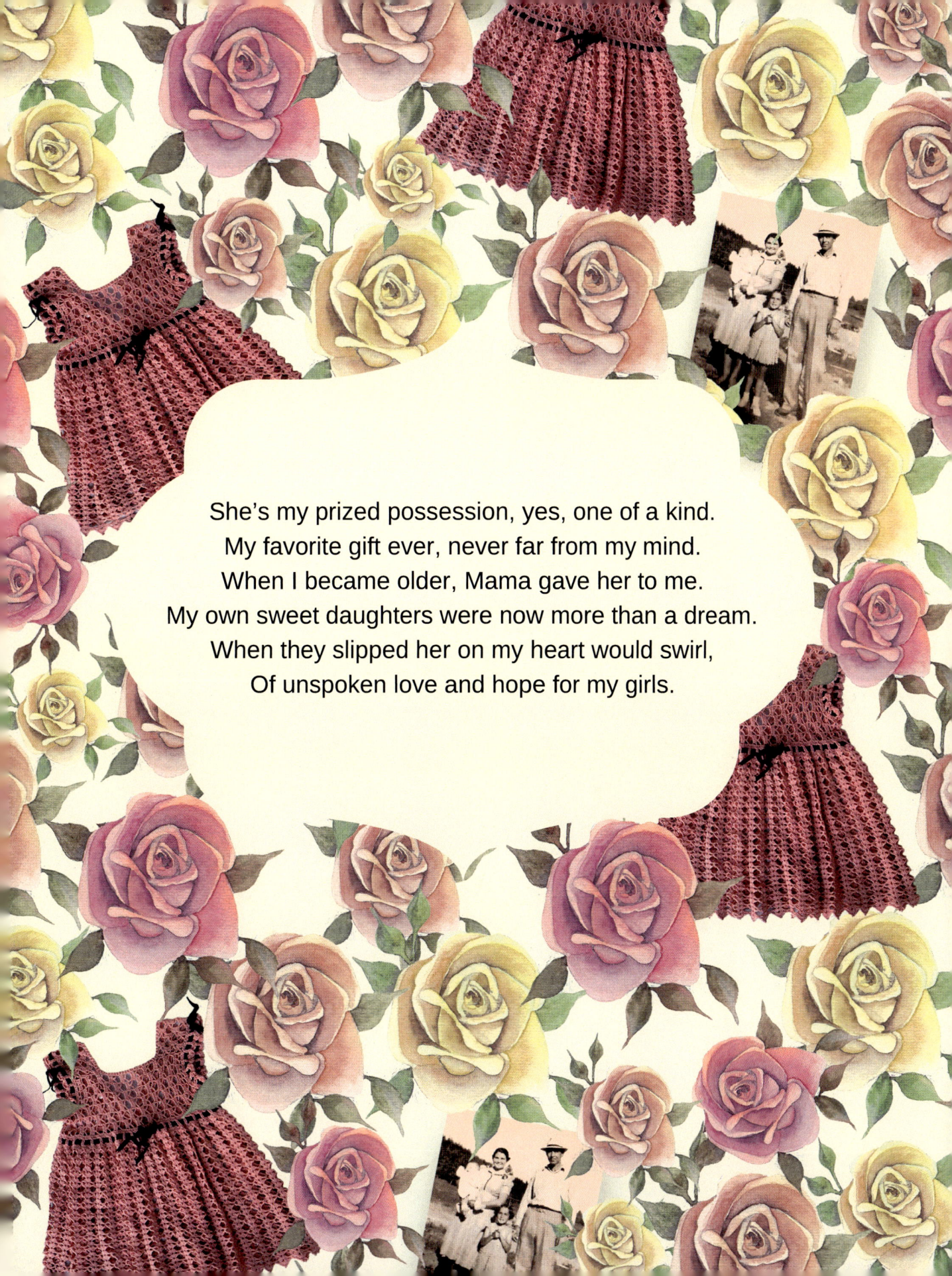

She's my prized possession, yes, one of a kind.
My favorite gift ever, never far from my mind.
When I became older, Mama gave her to me.
My own sweet daughters were now more than a dream.
When they slipped her on my heart would swirl,
Of unspoken love and hope for my girls.

My crocheted dress gifted to me,
Was full of love that I still can see.
She goes over your head and love fills up your heart.
That's how it's been...right from the start!
Like a cloak of love, strength, and grace,
Joy spins and swirls all over the place!

My daughters, I love you, and granddaughters to come.
I love you forever, each special one.
I hope that this story reminds you of me,
And the lady that blessed me and always could see...
That all little girls need...love, grace, and time,
It's a joy to share her with you in this rhyme.

Our tradition continues...

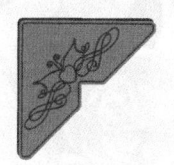
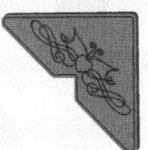

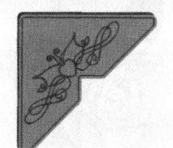

From the Author

Once upon a time my mother was given a very special gift. The year was 1940 and her baby brother was soon to be born. Right next door lived a generous eighbor who loved my mom, and crocheted a little dress for the big sister to be. My mother felt very special on the day that the dress was delivered.
As in every family with a baby on the way, attention in the household was shifting to the new delivery that soon would take place. But, my mother was remembered in a special way.

This dress became a big part of her childhood as she shared it with other little girls. Each girl would try on the crocheted dress and have their picture taken. We may not have all of the early photos, but when her daughters were born, mom made sure every girl's photo went in a special album. These photos were taken with all kinds of cameras. The 1940's folding camera complete with 620 film was likely the first camera to capture the crocheted dress. Later came 35-millimeter film, and of course digital-the images still tucked away on a hard drive! Most recently, the coral-colored dress and the smiles were captured on cell phones.

It was very important that all the girls in the family took their turn in my mother's one of a kind heirloom dress. The photo shoots only lasted a few minutes, but it meant the world to my mom to share this most delicate dress with all the little girls she loved. It represented how she was always remembered, even though her world was changing. Most importantly, it was to show that each little girl who wore that dress, was amazing in her own right. Mom would enjoy a second little brother some years later.

Maybe you have a tradition that makes a little girl in your world know her incredible worth. Or, maybe it's time to create memories of your own that will last for generations. Record the smiles...make the memories...love.

Michelle Lynae

Made in the USA
Monee, IL
27 February 2021